The Animals of Buttercup Farm

STORY BY

Judy Dunn

PHOTOGRAPHS BY

Phoebe Dunn

RANDOM HOUSE 🏠 NEW YORK

Photographs Copyright © 1981 by Phoebe Dunn. Text Copyright © 1981 by Judy Dunn Spangenberg. All rights reserved under International and Pan-American Copyright Conventions. Published in the United States by Random House, Inc., New York, and simultaneously in Canada by Random House of Canada Limited, Toronto.

Library of Congress Cataloging in Publication Data: Dunn, Judy. The animals of Buttercup Farm. SUMMARY: Describes the animals of Buttercup Farm and their activities throughout a typical day. 1. Domestic animals—Juvenile literature. 2. Farm life—Juvenile literature. [1. Domestic animals. 2. Farm life] I. Dunn, Phoebe. II. Title. III. Title: Buttercup Farm. SF75.5.D86 636 AACR2 81-4892 ISBN: 0-394-84798-9 (trade); 0-394-94798-3 (lib. bdg.)

Manufactured in the United States of America   2 3 4 5 6 7 8 9 0

All the children in the neighborhood like to visit Buttercup Farm. There are meadows and barns and barnyards to explore. But, best of all, there are lots of animals! The first thing the children do is visit the ponies in fields yellow with buttercups. Everyone always gets a free pony ride.

Farmer John's mare has just had her new spring foal. The foal looks funny trotting on his long, wobbly legs. But soon he will be galloping along with his mother.

The cows have their own pasture to graze in. They munch on grass all day long. The cows look like they are ready to be milked, thinks Farmer John.

The calves stay in the barnyard until they are old enough to join their mothers. Midnight, one of the barn cats, keeps them company. She gives a calf a friendly lick and the calf licks her back.

Farmer John has milked the cows in the barn, and now it is time for them to graze in the fields again. This newborn calf wishes she were old enough to go with them.

Farmer John rewards
the cats for catching
mice in the barn.
He saves a bucket
of warm, foamy milk
especially for them.

There are always lots of new kittens in the barn. They get their milk from their mother. The kittens are very curious about everything that is going on. Soon their mother will be teaching them how to catch mice with her.

Red hens and brown hens and speckled hens
all go cluck, cluck, cluck when they see
Farmer John coming.

First he feeds them,
and then he collects their
eggs in a wire basket.

This hen is still in her
nesting box. She has
just laid a warm brown
egg!

Tammy lives down the road from Buttercup Farm. She comes every day to feed her favorite chicken. Tammy has raised her since she was a little chick.

Tammy's chicken is very tame. She likes Tammy to carry her.

On the first sunny day of spring, mother hen
shows her chicks all the corners of the farm
and good hiding places under the blackberry
bush. Farmer John's dog is out playing, too.
The chicks go peep, peep all around him. He
wonders if they will be his friends.

The rooster struts around shaking his big red comb and showing off his fancy tail. He is sure that he is the king of the barnyard! The proud old gander parades up and down and honks at everything he sees. He thinks that *he* is the king!

The rest of the geese run back and forth inside their pen. Honk, honk! What a lot of noise they make! This goose has found a quiet spot to lay her eggs. Soon goslings will hatch.

The ducks love to swim
in the pond.

Mike thinks it would be
fun to give his pet duck a
bath. But first he has to
catch him!

The tiny pink piglets are all lined up for
lunch. They look like a row of piggy banks!
The mother sow is enormous.

She lies there patiently giving them her milk.
Oink, oink, they squeal, as they greedily
shove and push each other.

The mother sow is looking for her food now. She needs to eat a lot so she can make enough milk for all of her piglets. This little pig has had enough to eat. He is taking his nap.

Now it's time to play! All the brothers and sisters like to play piggyback, piggy-in-the-middle, and piggy-on-top.

They play all sorts of
piggy games until they are
hungry again!

There's a new litter of rabbits on Buttercup Farm.

They huddle around their mother inside the rabbit hutch. They are the quietest animals on the farm.

When they hear a noise, their long, pink ears stand up and wiggle. This rabbit turns around to see if his special friend is here.

Kate has come to pet him. She visits every day after school. At first the little rabbit was shy, but now he likes to be held.

All the other rabbits are
happy to see her, too.
She brings carrots and
lettuce for all of them.
When Kate has to leave,
her special friend stands
up to say good-bye.

The goats are very frisky today. They leap and butt each other and frolic in the tall grass. Ma-a-a-a, says a goat from his stall inside the barn. He wants to play outside, too.

Farmer John has a big flock of sheep. They graze in the fields with their new spring lambs. The sheep are still wearing their woolly winter coats. Soon it will be shearing time. Jodie's favorite animals are the little lambs. They always like to be cuddled.

One lamb was very small
and weak when he was
born. Emmy has been
taking good care of him.
Now he is almost as big
as the other lambs.

Soon he will be too big to
carry around. But he and
Emmy will always be good
friends.

"Good night, little lamb," says Emmy from the barn door. "I'll see you tomorrow." All of Farmer John's animals are inside now. They have had a long day and are ready for a good night's sleep. Tomorrow will be another busy day on Buttercup Farm.